Sanctuary

Martyn Halsall is a retired journalist, writing, reviewing and editing poetry at home in rural West Cumbria.

Sanctuary

Poems by
Martyn Halsall

CANTERBURY
PRESS
Norwich

Copyright © Martyn Halsall, 2014

First published in 2014 by the Canterbury Press Norwich
Editorial office
3rd Floor, Invicta House,
108–114 Golden Lane,
London EC1Y 0TG

Canterbury Press is an imprint of Hymns Ancient & Modern Ltd
(a registered charity)
13A Hellesdon Park Road, Norwich,
Norfolk NR6 5DR, UK

www.canterburypress.co.uk

British Library Cataloguing in Publication data

A catalogue record for this book is available
from the British Library

978 1 84825 675 0

Typeset by Regent Typesetting, London
Printed and bound in Great Britain by
CPI Group (UK) Ltd, Croydon

Contents

To Isobel:
wife, mother, teacher, priest;
who believed in it.

Preface

Cathedrals seem to be among the scarce places where church congregations are growing, perhaps because they offer place and worship for people to encounter God without being corralled into 'parish strategies', or dragooned into impersonating submarines or orang-utans in 'action songs'.

Cathedrals magnetise visitors without demanding immediate membership, and inherent commitment. They introduce the Christian past into the secular present, and patiently celebrate the presence of God in a society where s/he is felt often to be as redundant as a coal miner, or as optional as a poet.

Cathedrals intrigue, so people respond. They are generous in many ways, including their encouragement of discerning God through the arts. They take risks, often using the arts experimentally in creative theology, venturing into the radical and the prophetic.

They provide spiritual hospitality to the jaded; a place with the risen Christ to re-imagine the familiar, and dare fresh potential. They share space to renew and redeem lives, in the companionship of the Holy Spirit. They offer sanctuary.

Most of these poems reflect aspects of the life and faith of one cathedral. They were drafted, after a life in journalism, in a new role as the first Poet in Residence of Carlisle

Cathedral. Like journalism, they grew from notes, conversations, observations, reflections and experiences; from being there.

Prelude:
Leaving St Bridget's

Came the day and the master said: 'It's finished,
it's good work.' We all stepped back to look
up for once, as the priest was always asking.

What did he see? Not the callous under squared stone
lifted, set day after day. Not grey and grit
of mortar, not scaffold and winded hoist swaying

in a cross-raising, but high blues and whites
of Our Lady, and an angels' sky. We raised our eyes.

The master said: 'Time to be packing the carts, then
off to the next one.' First he let us wander
to see the whole thing, feel the others' work:

that angle in the arrowed door, that soar
of arch over altar, 'stone rainbow span'
as the priest described it; each frame of light

where we set eternity square. Each footstep
took us further away. One pause, to look back
at the scale of it, ship above the mill of huts,

then a bend in the lane. A stand of thinning ash
made a picket between us and our past. Four days
tramping churned roads through buffet and drench.

A Roman line to start, then a gesture of sea,
and gradually, when the sky stood back a bit,
a level of hills pegged true, like the new walls

we'd raise when we arrived, a dream in stone
built in St Mary's name. New Latin word,
and world: 'cathedra'.

Foreign Correspondent

You touch down, wondering about language,
your need for a translator, your contacts book
thin on the ground. You face deadlines to update
news running for centuries, to find a new
line beyond headlines of decline, or saviour.

You are set between last flight, next empty morning,
sit at the back, watch, attempt the low profile
of a holy visitor or resident angel, caught
between being yourself, and representing who sent you.

So many potential angles: those identities
carved for a screen, those poets poised by the door
for a quick exit, Jacobite prisoners, that idea of collecting
stars to roof the psalms, graffiti, translating runes.
You remember those sitting by phones, waiting for a
    story.

Close

Always surprised by gulls that call this city
awake, or scratch the morning with sharpened shrieks
that stretch over holy towers and overlapped lorries
offloading in delivery bays. Eternity's

still in the Close. A single cyclist sidles
shyly from Morning Prayer, unchains his bike;
a trio of schoolboys, uniforms trimmed to trend,
gossip by with identical bags, as advertised.

The copper beech alters its colour secretly
in slowly turning light; lichens become
green again in sun's reach, first thrush rehearses
his song, beyond organ practice muffled by sandstone.

Those passing stroll, outlined by sunlight, as
sound seeps through from the city's undertow.
Devotions could come outside this spotlit morning,
a sort of prayer cast into the shape of birdsong:

with reference to the gargoyles' twisted suffering,
rattle of a train that slows down after distance,
those passing with their needs, baggage, potential;
how shadow is moved by light, occasional voices

discussing the day ahead, nurse and dog-walker,
those listening in through headphones, the bowed heads
furrowing into busyness, and that capacity
for all prayer to surprise: sudden oystercatchers.

Akeland

I found the pencil, lost out in the Close,
lime stripe as straight as mown cathedral lawn,
sharpened to the point where its given Cumbrian name
had been reduced to 'akeland'. Its lead stayed

core, its power like a uranium rod,
potential as prayer that drives plea and direction,
drawn between blunt and point with use and sharpening.

I imagined it pocketed, taken North in parallel
to the masons' track, plumb-line from Durham to Orkney
to work the same liverish stone into cathedrals.

My voyage was rather North-west, out of Oban,
the pencil stowed away in a wax jacket pocket
to copy Gaelic into a notebook, seeking
'cathedral' among words for 'midge' and 'Indian takeaway'.

Here Lyeth Ye Bodys

The dead have their own quarter, ghost space
outside old walls that are no longer there;
moraine of names, gathered, eroded, sometimes
just a stump; brief essays in anonymity.

Here Lyeth Ye Bodys; identities planed down
by weather, and some black slates set flat
as steppings for a clapper bridge, as sentry;
one's stapled to the wall, moonscape in sandstone.

Most are *Sacred to the Memory of* ... yet often
flaked to prepositions, or a subtracted date.
One's cracked like a commandment tablet, a weed
arguing through the fissure. Moss fuzzes carving.

Some still shout in block capitals. Tiered marble castles,
fortifies THE EARTHLY REMAINS OF THE
    HONORABLE
SAMUEL WALDEGRAVE DD ... FELL ASLEEP IN
    JESUS
1869. *Remember those who have rule over you.*

A brief space for so many passing, ruled
over by patched buttresses that prop the wall,
a black fence spiked to an armoury, a beech
hedge rustling like page-turning cassocked choristers.

One's modest, a sandstone plinth with inset slate,
almost outside cathedral grounds, a body's
length from the cobbled street: *Robert Anderson
The Cumbrian Bard*, poet; saluted on the edge of things.

Gargoyles

The Guide's brief mention of grotesque, a photograph
more ink blot than detail, smudge than features,
'in the corbel table supporting the nave parapet'.

Parable by absence; the sceptic's version
of church history. Somewhere in the dark
a plague face, twist of features into pain,

caricature theology, a reversed healing,
some mason taking the piss with a dean's features.

Same loss or sadness or incompleteness
followed the day conference on war and child soldiers,
through the distribution of clay, shade of a suntan.

The face she made, with recesses for eyes and nose,
lop-sided twist of smile, tendency to topple,
could form a gargoyle in our wounded century.

Entrances

That line between three worlds, past, present, future,
thins over threshold; at the breath of a door,
footsteps sharpened on stone, a gasp of stars
that fill the roof, suggest a high perspective,
that builds infinity out of the perpendicular.

Each entering brings and takes. A photo-ticket
opens the electronic apertures to icons
on thumbnail sim-cards. Once journal note or sketch
had to contain all memories and perceptions,
a passing bonnet, cliffed walls; prayerful stillness.

Still somewhere to reach out; print words on silence,
make something out of apparent nothingness,
that mental mime where bowed heads conjure prayer,
that silent mail where cards are left by candles
posted to holiness, somewhere. This space

allowing those seeking to frame their own responses:
photographer's flash creating instant diaries,
a sanctuary pause inside the scurrying world;
some recognition, through light or space or echo
of something further, someone beckoning.

Runes

Following a flashlight, hoovering through the dark,
he found runes; twiggery, a woven stick fence,
predominantly verticals, and the odd curve
like a glance of sky between twin tower blocks,

a signed boast of sparse literacy at that time:
Dolfin wrote these runes on this stone.
Questions follow, as always when a light's switched off,
when anyone goes down from a high discovery:

Why did this man see need to sign the cathedral?
Why do the strokes grow longer with each rune?
Did confidence master suspicion of discovery?
Why the imperative to leave a name?

And why did the later schoolboys who made their marks
at choir practice need to bring their knives?
Thomas Pattinson, living at the sign of The Bush,
Robert Horsley, probably a butcher's boy.

Clues scribbled on scraps from eighteenth-century text
       books,
exercises, drawings, class-lists, found
in a fireplace unblocked two centuries later
continued that quiet ministry of cleaning, and disclosure.

Poets' Corner

Nicholson stands sentry, head and shoulders
above us as we enter, overlooking those
who do not glance up to spot him in recess,
as hacked black, out of coal; cold stare and muttonchops.

Lower, his companion's laid out in briefer words
than those he gathered in dialect: Robert Anderson,
the Cumbrian Bard, profiled in white marble.

Three footsteps in, floor flutters as the door opens,
a fan of light illuminates the slab
honouring Susanna Blamire, a 'poet of humour …
who caught the authentic voice of Cumberland'.

Together these compose Poets' Corner, a thin anthology,
more like theology where absence signals presence.

No Wordsworth, tidied away in Cockermouth,
Grasmere, Rydal. No Coleridge – missing, as usual.
No Southey, with his withered laurel of laureateship;
Tennyson and Ruskin dismissed among rejection slips.

Perhaps poets and too much certainty don't get on?
Or perhaps, like Duffy, their language is 'secular prayer',
echoes and side-glances; tentative, wary of entrance?

Re-entering Afghanistan

We keep returning; to bow, to kneel, to sing;
enlisting in the Military Chapel, joining up
for the weekly Eucharist for Peace and Justice.

Temptation is absence without leave, to pass by
casualty lists entrenched in marble and brass,
that gradual democracy from only officers' names

and 'four drummers and 289 privates' between
draped flags to a whole roll-call, set among wreaths.
Not only those 'Killed in Action', but also, double,

those who 'Died of Disease'. Move on. Slow-march,
remembering the gold lettering 'in memory of all ranks',
geography of wired ground: Trench Warfare.

Behind the advance, school registers, confirmation classes
seeding such memorials across a grieving country. Imagine
those stepping back into a wider space as might

someone after laying a wreath, hearing a bugle.
Look up at the parade of names around the screen,
Relief of Ladysmith, Gallipoli, Landing in Sicily,

each dated as if we might forget that time.
And under angled glass, three open books where someone
comes weekly to turn the pages listing fresh alphabets

and numbers, and the chiming tone of all
the giving, and killing, and what continues:
Iraq, Iraq; re-entering Afghanistan.

Jetsam

Now high and dry, dredgings and recoverages
from the plunged cathedral well lie on display
like jetsam, once thrown overboard, fished out.

The unstated keeps them deep, their mysteries
blank as glass walls on their unlettered display case;
something locked in; those ancient keys, pickled in rust.

Lost property or discarded city history,
some underwater evidence, what's survived
from Noah's holed pockets, if he'd had small change:

this third-hand Charles the Second copper farthing,
or short-cross half-penny from the Durham mint,
or long-cross penny dating from the fourteenth century.

Physics has governed what's left, what's disappeared,
nothing soluble or edible, blot on charter
or gristle from a chop, yet Samian ware

or lead seal from Estonian linen order,
clay pipe-bowl, inch-lengthed decorated stems
are laid out with wig-curlers for inspection.

When looking down the telescope of shaft
to eventual water, as here, we find ourselves
trembling in a hidden and distorting current,
wondering if what we own makes who we are.

St Antony and the Projectionists

(a screen)

Some have lost faces, bit-players in the life
of St Antony, outlined on varnished panels.
He exchanged wealth for a desert hermitage
'without any company save the wild boar'.

Split timbers show his miracles; discovering a well
for monks dying of thirst, walking on water,
ordering wild animals to hew a cave,
being healed by Christ after a devils' ambush.

No healing for those stripped of their faces
in the Great War. Some were given masks.
Others found jobs as cinema projectionists,
too shocking to be seen, supervising fantasies

in fluttering black and white, hearing talkies arrive
alongside memories of wailing shells. A few, too few,
might have made their way back to this cathedral,
finding in Antony's screen ammunition box splinters,

in his hands the courageous rescue of stretcher bearers,
among the demons, those shrieking in No Man's Land,
among church visitors the silhouettes of a wire-party,
in and out of a Spring day's searchlight sunlight.

Antony remains alert, his night-watch eyes
sentry over the pedestrian; sack truck, fire-hose, a folding
table like a preparation of wood, nails, bayonets
for the re-enactment of sacrifice among the onlookers.

Mirror

Look down, and you see stars, an angled mirror
lifts you from the nave to the indoor galaxy
shaping the ceiling. It is clearer here,
easier to see each patterned frame than standing back
crooking your neck, trying to decipher

patterns and award a name. Among the identical
they are all different, given angles of light,
yet not near enough to identify, no Plough, Orion's
Belt, Dog Star; too few for a Milky Way,
too young to twinkle. Presence in absences

like that yearning for the discreet God
some Russian theologians muse about.
Ironic that we approach them at ground level.
But, come Advent, dusk, someone might stay
to watch in case a new star rises; moves.

Estimating Zechariah

(from the effigy of Bishop Samuel Waldegrave)

The Bishop floats, the same alabaster as iceberg
seen from the air; adrift, a prayerful backstroke,
his head propped by some cushions or a sort
of swimming aid, his robes furrowed like a glacier.

No evidence of drowning, rather marble rest,
the face of a sleeper, the shoulders sagged from bearing
burdens of offices, scholarship, that prayer
that may have echoed back, seeming unanswered.

Study him; his slack right hand turned down,
his left closer to his heart, wrapped over
a book, a finger crooked in like a bookmark,
presumably his Bible, perhaps the final verse

read before nightfall. We try to gauge the place
and estimate Zechariah, and remember
that sermon planed like pine boards on an island,
its mystery of myrtle trees, and coloured horses.

Rest now, in the peace promised in chapter one.
Is the presence of the messenger decoded;
the symbolism addressed – no marble boat,
but something of angel, his vision gathering wings?

Ribs

(from the memorial to Bishop John Bardsley)

He brought sea with him: John Wareing Bardsley,
translated from Sodor and Man, a Viking crossing,
his memorial part shield, part cartwheeling waters,

black metal that chimes to the knuckle of a knock,
and slate where his oared boat made a tilt at mooring,
the crest of a wave breaking over obituary:

A Man of Rare Humility and Loving Kindness
flanked by simple mourners, John Baptist off the fell,
and a barefoot servant girl, stilled by the company.

Swirls at the North edge, flaring to a whale's tail,
and in the deep the black fangs of an anchor.
A footnote *Concern for the poor*, and a mooring rope.

We turn North towards today's iced wind. A bell
summons to the Eucharist for Peace and Justice
in a splintered half-ring, cross-section of chairs like ribs

of a candlelit longboat out of Man for mainland.
Wafer raised like a globe to preach a parable,
the broken pieces passed among the few

who come to pray for change, and to be changed
as turning shield to sail, and rib to voyage.

East Window

That same climbing on one another's shoulders
as in some Spanish village during fiesta;
same tapering, though not upwards to the lightest child
but stoppered by doctrinal weight of Christ in Judgement.

He's powerful, alone, the pinnacle
of village folk that Chaucer would have relished,
noting same velvet robes, rough cloaks; same sticks
and swords he'd pass in any squeeze of side-street,

or watch through tale and tramp on pilgrimage.
Used faces, cast as angels, shepherds, gamblers,
bridegroom, his anxious steward, virgin, kings

dressed up to take a part, pageant in glass,
contemporary, modern-dressed medieval light;
same weight in air as pictured in crucifixions.

Fag Break

(from the black and white photograph 'Fag Break at the Undercroft, Carlisle Cathedral, 1981' by Eric March)

Judging by her headscarf, almost a novice wimple,
and the out of focus community in the background,
she works here; serves scones, pours tea, washes dishes.
But she's come out, pausing in vocation to chat
to someone out of sight, like prayer, on a fag break.

Something has caught her attention. Her eyes are bright
like peering into conspiracy, her cigarette's
overlooked for a moment, her lighter flat
on the snapped-back packet. 'What was that she said?'

Smoke drifts off like a sacristan with a snuffer.
She's discarded her vow of silence to answer back.
Nothing too holy, perhaps, but given the date:
'She's going to do what? So where are our rights, for
    God's sake?'
Her blouse is a trellis in summer. She senses frost.

Haiti

New architecture; grey against kidney sandstone,
flat below an arch's leap, not built to last
longer than a charity reminder about Haiti.

An egg box house, low roof pitch of white paper,
sellotape over a tear, someone has counted
one three eight five, not as a medieval date

but totalling the needed pounds to fund such places,
replacing earthquake ruins. Brown sticky tape
holds it together, like a prayer for hope.

Smell of dry cardboard, 13-digit barcodes,
trade names appear on honeycombed papier mache:
South Lakeland Free Range, Church and Manor Farm.

A door's built, green, like a glimpse of open country,
Four-by-five window, deep yellow as a yolk:
Eggs from Caged Hens, see inlid for more details,

and children had responded in poems and posters
having brought their box and pound to fund such places:
The people in Haiti were heart break,

after the event they hardly spoken …
All you could hear was cries and yells
and the ever-lasting sound of bells.

Sparse lighting; spotlights stare down at statistics:
220,000 people killed, 300,000 injured,
one million left homeless; 500 families re-housed.

New architecture: rescuers' blue and white
Mary the Virgin colour scheme; among official shelters
two burned-out helicopters become accommodation,
and a bell answers, summoning the Mass for Justice.

Meeting Gabriel

Spiral into pealing; wedged steps lead
up to a giddy gallery above the nave.
Higher than carved angels' choir; liana hemp
is pulled for the final corkscrew to the ringing chamber.
Twelve ropes are lowered, noosed. Air's stilled.

Something of a ship: creaked rigging and plain timbering,
a sense of voyage as five tons of sound
are raised for pealing. Also red depth of stone
where six-foot walls are patterned with diamond light
that evening threads through glass. Time's poised.

Pairs of hands grip each sally. A slipped leash
    announcement:
'Treble's going; she's gone'. Everyone follows.
The handstroke's pulled to keep the music taut;
a slight bounce, and the tailend of the rope
is held at head height, keeping the bell in balance,
pulled again, bounced; sally's caught, gripped again.

Changes are called. 'Five over six ... four over seven ...
six over two ...' A tremor's inside the tower,
rattling of ropes, an underlying rumble, sound billowing
following the liturgies of columned numbers: Antelope,
Union, Stedman's Slow Course, Grandsire,
Double Oxford, Duffield; equations of Surprises.

Domestic among symphonic, round-shouldered jackets
drape on an old half-bell wheel, tissues, mints
join each bell named from saints, inscribed, and blessed,
Bega: 'Hastings and Constance Rashdall gave me to God.'
Maria, retired, hangs silent after six centuries.

The whole air's flocked with ringing, filling distance
glimpsed through the slit glass, stretched to distant fells.
Each order's brief: 'Bob Doubles, two plain courses'.
Single word 'Stand' brings each course to its end.
Each rope's looped, hovers in the aftermath.

And someone asks if the trumpeter has come
to improvise his jazz, solos off sandstone
hundreds of feet below, riffing off bells,
fanfare and echo, like an angel's meeting.

Sanctuary

She towed her trolley, hubble-bubble, over cobbles
and entered the cathedral through the door with a hiss.
She waited for deafening Amenning echoes to fade.

New words bombasted in the language of stone and brass,
long military roll calls under bats' wing creak of flags;
the *The* in the slate floor that followed her everywhere.

So many dead in the dust were announcing themselves.
She flinched, preferring candles with their tongues of fire.
She heard half-remembered singing, and went to hide

backstage, behind the altar. Men were emerging
out of the walls, chanting their status and rank:
Bishop, Archdeacon. A Great Servant of the State.

She watched a woman crouching under dead weight
of murmuring among arches that propped medieval air.
She saw that her lips barely moved, and knew she made

the same sounds as voices clamouring in her head,
sometimes from the powerbrokers, sometimes from
      memories
that inspired the saint by the lake at work on his prayers

whose eye she caught in stained glass; who understood.
She knew he would stay by the water with its lap and beat,

and bring her the stillness of beech trees that answered
   back

only in breathing, that hosted absolving birds.
She went outside, and found the whole city miming,
except for the daughter spelling *Welcome*, in sign
   language.

Outsider

Late for Evensong, somewhere between
responses and Magnificat. She chose to stay
the far side of the closed screen where
the inside dusk was parsed with candlelight.

She turned a chair among the slate memorials
to masculine wars, for a gold glimpse of the altar,
a high, blue portion of the rooflit stars:
heard of the meek that God would elevate.

She left The Creed to others, kept her anger
silent in cathedral's shuffled prayer and psalm.
A canon led God's thanks for women clergy
(no word of bishops, night after the vote).

She watched the choir in green robes drain to echo.
She found night gathered outside, to share her exile.

The Line

Starting a long way back: a vaulted memory,
sound stained with incense through electric twilight;
yet still the occasional trip within the history,
storm crackling round the edge of antiphons.

Learning: not just a pause within the ethereal,
but starting to re-read the familiar, taking
note as a preacher might unfold a text
to seek its context, allowing it breathing space.

So that the line, shadowed like an underlining,
slipped from its page to cast a tarnished light
over the brass cross, sang what we dared not say,

was naked: *Take not Thy Holy Spirit from us*
made all the responses shiver, explained the occasional
side glance, latch to an exit; chill through the world.

First Reading

In the beginning that warning
of a weather system building out
in The Atlantic, the Genesis territory,

where only slicked lift and fall of ocean
was sensed in the invisible night,
and the only sounds smelled of salt.

Exiles wrote first about ocean,
then a garden, and in failing light
God, lonely among woodland,

calling: 'Where are you?'
For that moment they hung up their lyres
knowing that across endless water

there is rarely a reply, or
one that can be heard through
oiled turmoil. Later they learned

to decode isobars and occluded fronts
as reading the rings on a tree,
as adding a postscript,

God again, lonely in a garden
asking: 'Could you not watch
with me, just for an hour?'

The Redundant Psalmist's
Sudoku Theology

You come to the end of music. Someone says:
We've enough psalms. Words like *redundancy*
or *down-sized* are poised, like the buzzard overhead
spiralling, re-drafting circles. You begin again,

searching for threes, Trinity in these new days,
like cracking open a sudoku, prising crosswords loose,
or opening an oyster, and finding flesh
in the arc of pearl, that's dark and tastes of ocean.

So a psalm hovers. That same incompleteness
that kept us awake, that force eight battering ram,
unlit express tearing through churchyard lime trees;
a flailing world, trying to find some way home.

As writers we're all over the place. Anger
overflowing like the last round, soured
with fear, besieged by anxieties. Yet
still the line jostles through: *You are our Father*.

January: another five days until the holly and ivy,
already wilting after the open fires,
come down for another year. We find
the Son changing; a child becoming difficult.

Death threat seems to follow him, suddenly
that quick light over snow, that last response
that stays on: *Take not Thy Holy Spirit from us.*

Evensong: three of us between the choir and clergy,
two in the roosts of canons' stalls, that woman
headscarved and swaddled against winter, with her
   shopping trolley,
glancing round, to check that we are still with her.

On Preaching

As you climb to speak you are conscious of cruelty,
of carvings of shackled men that support the pulpit
turning it into a slave ship. Why did the Dutch masters
chisel this imagery? Why do the hearers come?

The danger is in looking down. You glance
as someone might catch details of hands
releasing a catch on a pigeon basket, might
nod like bidding for an argument, as sensing breeze change.

No-one can look away. They are facing you,
or at least lined to your direction, like writing
that confronts you; those ancient texts
that cannot be by-passed, that demand negotiation.

Yet all the time you are conscious of sailing,
feeling the world sway, as from a crow's nest.
Are listeners expecting answers? Have they brought
questions, or simply that habit of returning with an olive
    leaf?

Lighthouse

Glance up again, and the light's
moved, now striping cathedral stonework
behind the preacher, part of the sculpture,
part of his illumination. He speaks about

that Prayer Book revolution, from the hidden
priest celebrating a Mass in a distant
language, out of sight behind
a screen, whispering, out of earshot,

accompanied by not so much
a congregation as individuals, milling
around with their separate prayers,

to today's community, communion,
eucharist. He stands high as a lighthouse.
In the last hymn, sunlight's risen
almost to carved angel height,
without us noticing.

Congregation

*(after Another Place, Crosby beach, Merseyside,
by Antony Gormley)*

Ebb; and they rise again, their steeled
bodies a sheen of rust and brine, recovering
air after a submarine journey, each
nameless, despite baptism, each numbered
by a tag on the wrist. Each face
a mask across the sea's movements,

and effects. Textures in close-up show
green peel of a cheek, thumb's oxidised
leprosy, pebbles and shells crotched
into rubbled shadows, a leotard of weed,
an askew wig of gull shit, sand-blasted stare,
saline basting of a chest; then out

over a half-continent of sand and water,
creeks, runnels, channels, foundries of shallows
to parallels of coastlines and the eventual
hills. Low tide, and they have all emerged,
each facing the estuary, listening for curlews,
hands open for nets, as if to land light.

None speaks. They leave the gift of tongues
to each interpreter. Perhaps they are waiting
to depart; for the space ship or longboat to appear,
or a high enough tide to lift them as they are? Somehow
they might reach into breast stroke, become Atlantic.

Shadowlands

Part of the great cathedral has disappeared,
secreted into shadow by an irony of floodlights;
North Transept become matt block, the parade
of buttresses halved along the wrong side of dusk.

Inside some wait in a patchwork of shadowlands,
circle dance of candelabra, a candle's star,
stilled rookery of regimented flags, chipped marks
in columns, deepened, height of a wall sliced off.

Three bells, some distant singing, first responses;
starched shuffle of the choir and two priests
climb to their stalls for Evensong. They seem
to have come through a distant country for this liturgy.

Seven choristers lead versicles and responses,
a single chord sets the warm key for the psalm
hoisted between voices like a shuttlecock.
Light leaks through cracks in boards, lays stripes on flags,
lodges as yolk below a choir lamp,

defines a surplice crease. Same verticals
as giddy towards the rack of angels' roost.
Ribbed plaster's printed with the diamonds patterned
through matt, short-sighted glass that weather grained.
A trace remaining after lights go out,

flicker after blessing. Silence not really silence,
tallow chant lingering after a candle's blown.
Someone stays, listening, after the choir's passed
the glistening cross, overhears sound more like
a creak of hidden footsteps within dark carving.

Crossings

News from your Hebrides is often weather,
ferry delayed by gale, again; I imagine
a boat edging out of the shelter of the island,
the strew of lights from hamlets and the odd
croft falling astern. Perhaps a clearing of stars
gradually mapping a passage after the storm.

East, we still sit under tempest, hear again
Christ's summons to the impossible, same order
onto the waves; his overthrow of waters.

No map across the cathedral; its night crossing
no more than a protective footstep, sudden flicker
of shadow, the way a stripped bough moves outwith
stained windows. But earlier, same story starting
Advent, and that daily passage, vergers, guides,
those coming to follow in faith's footsteps,
those coming to wonder about story, storm, and forecast.

Catching the Greys

One story tells of a juggler, most of his bright
globes aloft at any one time, being caught
performing his art before Our Lady's statue;
and all the authorities who turned him out,
and all the scandalised audience, missing the point.

Yet in the same essence of silence a weaver sat,
perhaps with the click of his craft as the shuttle drew
skeins into rainbow design as his prayer became
a tapestry that gathered skeins of light.

Also, the woman, using the most discreet space
to set out her tools of water jar, palette, brush,
small sketchbook of that paper with gritty texture,
to track the elusive – dusk, the sigh of God,
his presence through this pewtered, winter light.

On Unicorns

(Psalm 22.21 King James Version)

Only ever a glimpse, like a flinch, flint strike
in a singe of horse hair, tail wind like wisped smoke
that a candle leaves when a rogue draught blows it out;
a horseshoe print of sound in a single note.

Only a fleeting canter of word in a psalm
like a memory or wraith deep among winter woods;
no origin or destination; only a named
recollection of something similar in a child's book.

Horn down and pounding leaf mould in slow motion,
muffled drum. Quickly the choristers had moved on,
high voices among psalm's images like a bleached stone.
Perhaps he was only ever a myth, though someone

saw him, as part of a herd, was transfixed, felt
fear from the ring of spears, cried out.
Later he returned to honour through a poet's debate,
that lifting of pierced hands, and the desolate

appeal of a writhing, bloodied, abandoned Christ
who might have shared unicorns' evenings in the desert.
Only ever a footnote in the scholar's draft,
extinct after translation by the Stuarts,

so they became 'wild oxen' in modern text;
still dangerous, but snuffing down their poise and
   lightning,
like listing the Holy Spirit as an afterthought:
same shutting of a chancel door, after the bolting.

Ark

Unicorns stayed on, stowed away in a psalm,
and rarely noticed among the cathedral's creatures,
scattered after the rainbow faded, and ground dried.

Something seems to move in the ancient glass
reassembled to an abstract light, a patch of fleece
or hint of mole or badger in a shuffle of moonlight.

Yellow wings, perhaps all that's left of a fox's kill,
and whatever is shadowed and rustling through oak
   woodland;
some evidence of a cloven print, a horn shaft?

Under each canon's seat a dark cruelty
is carved within the stories of misericords;
a dragon is swallowing a man in a short tunic,

a boar is savaging a rock band roadie's shoulder,
a serpent's entwining a deer, fox dragging a goose;
two geese killing an eel, two fawns witnessing a murder.

On panels are modest otters Cuthbert watched,
other creatures without ambition; an ox behind Mary
that watched her son born, stood still, chewing it over.

Some horses, saddled and bridled, in a Flemish carving,
being ridden to a crucifixion past the eel-sellers
through a panelled side-street as if this was an ordinary
    Friday.

Perhaps, during storms threatening to float the church,
the lions still roar around the Military Chapel,
descend from their coats of arms with the green gryphon?

Or there's gale-force wingspan among dragons,
wind roar of angels on stallions? Today, outside,
darkening gulls tilt in a sky slate overhung with rain
    warning.

Staying in Air

Some never returned to the ground, after the flood,
but stayed in air, and there the masons found them,
revealed from stone that formed the capitals
as oak forest, where pillars changed to woodland.

Gradually a frontier company, an outlaw alliance,
a certain cruelty, an owl with its murderous beak
clamped to a mouse's backbone, a fugitive
high among boughs – a hand yanking his goatee.

Two horses, wrestling and biting in a swaying crown,
an angel sleeping something off, a dog
impersonating a hunchback, a bear shambling forward
with basket and flagon; a villein unearthing a vixen.

The birds have flown from many boughs, become
a dragon with an abbot's head, its tail
hosepiping three columns, or left like the confused
eagle with a soldier's head, prophet's query of beard.

Strange music: a drunken fiddler has fled to this forest,
with a dreaming drummer and a tumbler shaping
     a question.
Silence: a woman has drawn the muffle of her hood
over her mouth to filter the rumour of a plague year.

Through the gap in a woodland acre, an eerie quiet;
leaves part to a stare, wide eyes of a Green Man
sentry in thicket as if assessing wood-carving,
the felling and shaping; theology of ransacked weather

itself become stone, like dragons' kiss, squirrel scutter
among its acorn harvest. The paradox of heaven
those seek by looking up, yet finding
a detaining verdict, guilt lingering among creation.

The Shopping of the Magi

Parking was a nightmare; three camels were tethered to
   choir stalls,
and all the hay was grazed from the starlit manger.
A cathedral verger was sent out for buckets, and shovels.

Then police turned up, about some visa problems.
Then the visitors asked for their crowns to be stored in
   the Treasury.
Then the gift shop had to be opened before they would
   leave.

Shopping list: probably a toddler from an ordinary sort
of family, so, no, not bookmarks of the cathedral's icon
as possibly not great readers, or reproduction carvings

of a dragon scratching its ear, or teddies in choir robes,
or even the Hedgerow Jelly made with Port, although
the 22-carat gold china caused some interest.

And the Hadrian's Balm ('contains pure beeswax'), but
they were thinking of serious metal – surely some crosses
could be melted down? And incense, for funeral
   arrangements?

Their visit was raised by the Bishop, under Overseas
    Mission.
Their apology for their attendants – that real ale, the
    night club –
was noted. The Welcome Sheet was tweaked to Persian.

Even the Holy Socks had failed to entrance them,
though the ceiling's galaxy provided directions.
For all the warmth of the welcome they had not come back;
something about angels, and going home a different way.

Nine Carols: Part-song

In cathedral darkness behind us, a child's cry,
raw, out of key, and set in a time of violence

in conflict with those settled for the opening carol
shuttlecocked between voices from Crossing to High Altar.

Occasionally it will intrude again, this announcement,
among the readings of a census summons, journeys,

prophecies, those angels striking wonder,
and terror, familiar trappings of well-rehearsed story,

like a blood-stain soaking into stone; chilled music
in several languages, open for our Amen.

Some will only imagine the embarrassed parents behind
that screen, carved into pinnacled crowns

of thorns, trying to silence their child
in case he intruded into the words and music;

or the mother opening one of the books
with the whole story, as her child slept,

and finding at the end a blank white page;
her own space, to complete the part-song.

Olaf's Nativity

No historian wrote it this way, but consider
this might offer a possibility; a priest,
named after his saint and king, is bedding down
for the night on rushes, amid the rustling mice
in small shelter – more a barn than chapel;
and wind is testing the latch, and sleet's forecast.

He had recognised this place; same verticals
as rock walls above fjords where his steps began.
His sailors had turned salt ribs, before they left,
from a spare boat into beams that roof his church.
So cloud became surf, his sanctuary a boat in sky;
and cold is seeping into stone, and the hearth's struggling.

Imagine him, settled in sleep, when a rough staff batters
oak shuttering him from dark. As he boils water,
trims a wick, rouses fire, tries to be discreet,
he waits for the shepherd's wife to assist the birth,
their first, as promised, to be named after a king.
And cloud's clearing high crags, and stars are praising.

Yew

A farmer reached for his carving tools, began
shaping from yew the cast list of Nativity;
shepherds and three wise men with gifts,
a donkey, parked camel, and a spare collie dog
that had wandered out of the night, and into history.

Three became one in the centre of the shed,
the father in a sort of teaching gown,
Edwardian hairstyle, more of an Oxford don
than expert with chisels that the farmer knew.
He shields his wife with downward arms, before
    cock-crow.

And she's intent; whole world a pool of a face
just visible in the shielding folds of her lap,
still part of her. Her face softened with thought
of whom this child could be, and where he might
travel and gather others with his teaching.
Her quiet recognition of his secret.

Still visitors come; lords, shepherds and carpenters,
others who watch to see if the figures move
or note how varnish enhances the flow of a cloak,
how a knot forms a scab to blemish a camel's hump,
reminder of all the miles, burden and wear.
Dark mark on a crown, going home by a different route.

Wild grain's disclosed in this typical churchyard tree,
lunch stop for fieldfares, redwings flocking together
to the southern side of winter. Planed shoulders are
  cloaked,
muscles varnished in opened arms offering a casket;
a wondering face, puckered to a question mark,
reflecting in the teardrop portrait of the baby.

Scene's set in straw, on sacking. Slatted wall's North,
thin shielding from a January in Cumbria,
open to the South's thin, winter light. Brief flames
from candles lit as prayers list from the draught
yet animate each yew face, reflect their searching.

Two Kings

They still return, sit on opposite sides of The Close.
One chooses Middle East sun to nod and dream
of how it all began, their long winter journey
ending with his gift, a sealed casket for anointing.

The other prefers shade, one foot drawn up on steps,
hands clasped around his knee as once on pommel,
as guarding the dark gift he brought for burial
never dreaming it would come to this, bus pass, and
    shopping trolley.

They do not glance or speak; that misunderstanding
on the road home, myopic misreading of night sky,
lingers, and differing theories of life and death
keep them apart. And neither of them hears

about the third, who brought gold, just that he found
sanctuary in wild places, re-defining kingdoms.

The Night Watch

(after Rembrandt)

Silence has the cathedral to itself.
Litany is echo; psalm beyond Amen.
Everything is stripped to essence, like the altar,
skeletal, table again, with minimum candles.

After the Maundy Eucharist, The Watch;
a scatter of people almost absorbed into darkness.
No words, now; just the shift of a crease
of a coat, the scrape of a chair, the shape
of genuflections, as a couple leave,

slipping like a wandering mind to an Amsterdam
side-street, finding a pour of men overflowing
out of a door to a drum-rattle, rag-bag militia;
top hats and helmets, pikes shouldered at all angles,
following a part-time colonel dressed in sunlight.

The cathedral is also a Rembrandt palette; gold
under lamps, a crimson brushstroke round
the empty crown or halo over the altar. Frays
of shadows, or light picked out in a starch of white,
the small cloth over the host; body under snow.

Nothing is quite what it seems; it appears
this Thursday is darkness leading into execution.
High names in illegible gold are old campaigns,
same trade as shamblers in the painted street scene:
text honouring all who died with the Border Regiment.

Night chill increases; a woman draws up her hood,
sits closer to herself. Bell counts eleven.
Memory picks out the captain with the blood-red sash
opening his hand to spotlight as if to nail
an aspect of belief. It was afternoon,
possibly Thursday, or Friday, in the original.

Drawn Swords

She senses them coming through the trees
with their drawn swords. Patches of evening
flickering gold, blood-red among the black.
As she hunches to kindle her prayers she remembers
so many swordsmen in their stained glass lights.

Time creaks through hours of the Watch, not yet quite
    Friday;
the aftermath of desertion. In leaded spaces
daylight marks out as windows, she knows they are
    waiting,
haloed, medieval knights, silvered in armour,
velvet cloak, sheepskin mantle, named as warriors:

'Jerubbaal who is Gideon', with his drawn sword,
dwarfing Victorian troopers with reversed arms,
Military Chapel icon of a Victoria Cross,
its liturgy, Sevastopol Peninsula. She shifts, slightly,
her hand touching the draught, hears scrape of a chair
or perhaps blades being unsheathed as medieval troops

in the great East Window settle for the night
to guard a borrowed tomb. Door eases like a sigh,
or St Oswald's breathing, arriving cross-gartered
and dressed for battle, his drawn sword resting
on his shoulder as three men raise a cross.

When she returns, in light, she will find the replica
of a sword that butchered Becket taken from the alcove
like a body removed by dawn. Instead, a garden
of daffodils, anemones, three empty crosses, tracks
in small flints pathed from a hill to an emptied sepulchre.

A Case for Dragons

Just because we are different ... pioneer
aeronauts, firebrands, our sense of entitlement to arson,
our butchery stench, our overshadowing wingspans,
our ability in leathery creaks to subdue whole
    landscapes ...

Admittedly, there were problems with golden damsels.
'It's in the genes,' I told my patient counsellor
in Conflict Resolution before I was banned over fire
    regulations.

I concede we were often seen as anti-social:
our liking for high air, propensity for caves,
and we had our image problems. We are usually found
in stained glass under a knight's foot, purple, and looking
queasy, with an Anglican lack of bloodstains.

While old George, crisp as a sprig out of Eton, would
    be all
gold helmet and halo, no gore on his surplice, more
    red crosses
than a BNP race riot, and a radio transmitter of a lance.
    I met
his comrade, years later, burger lunch on a park bench,
    his palfrey

grateful for some local authority grass. 'No hard feelings,
   mate,'
he said. 'It's probably over. You knew chivalry was
   privatised?
Me? I get by with supermarket openings, and the odd
heavy metal video.' He looked rusty; offered me his hand,
new meeting of claw and gauntlet; some warmth between
   them.

Resurrection: Evening Prayer

Supposing Christ came back, again, and found
these temple stones, also given resurrection,
these sandstone flags well-trod, all light
filtered through tall cascades of coloured glass,

and sat, still, waiting for silence to grow up
to something more. Perhaps some visitors' careful
footsteps, treading cautiously through stillness,
following the promise of something waiting to happen?

Someone might point to a notice saying Service Times,
perhaps hours away. Someone might prepare books
nearer those advertised times, and light high candles,

point out the whiteness of flowers arranged for Easter.
Supposing he sat for a while, remembering,
watching light weave on stone, graceful as obedience?

Resurrection: Night Bus

He wondered about leaning forward on the night bus
to warn the lad's shoulder, as he had touched her knee,
to say: *Look, she's not interested.* He feared a flare
like the back of a Roman hand; another blade.

She seemed to be coping, texting on regardless
of *Heys* and *You know, I was going to call.*
He saw his own face, anxious, reflected in windows,
slipping over privet and semis as the suburbs thinned

into matted country; the surge and rattle jolting
last handful of them, the night now passing in black
wherever he looked. The distance increasing between

stops, by a barn, near a lamp. The driver laughed
when he asked about Nazareth. *This is the 600, mate!*
He steadied scarred hands on the empty seat in front.

Quartets

(from Matthew Mark Luke and John No.1 *by Inigo Ford, in St Michael and All Angels' Church, Nether Wasdale, Cumbria)*

Resin blocks cupped in tissue squeal as bows
are primed with cello. A viola, two violins,
are wedged between shoulder and chin, as sighting
to take aim at the scores. The cello's plucked
to heartbeat. Glance stills a final twittered tuning,
discord, before a bow into the Mozart.
Behind them colours breathe through evening glass.
Christ's purple victory robe; a dawn's smashed yolk-light.

All evening translations: Janacek's 'Intimate Letters'
opened to imaginations: an angler's line
tightening; fields leaning from an evening train,
tossed blossom before a storm, breeze airing
a hammock, owl over graveyard. Music's guided
through nods, raised eyebrows, unthreading of a loose
horsehair … Behind them evening drains
light out of glass; turns angels to lead profiles.

Oak could have slept, or ascended into fire,
but four beams, rescued, were brought here, became abstract
portraits of writers: Matthew, Mark, Luke and John
Number One. And the artist asked his friends
what colours the apostles speak in, worked to grain

medical white for Luke, spread sky for John,
debtors' blue-black for Matthew, bloodied stripe
for Mark, and a tip of sunrise over a peg.

Night, and the figures from the glass manuscript
have stepped back into dark before resurrection.
No Christ, yet; or pair of angels with furled wings,
no sky-lined local ridge, slated from Wasdale,
re-sited to a Palestinian garden.
Just four men's names, called out with number and pack,
who never came home, but live on as east light
returns each dawn to make creation live.

Who gave their lives in the Great War: Jos Cooperthwaite,
Geo Cooperthwaite, Hugh R. Park, Walter K. Roper.
Next day's lament still echoes Shostakovitch.
Church door's left wedged to birdsong. Lambing's started.

R. S. Thomas Visits the Cathedral

Probably not; you cannot imagine him
responding to the guide's *Good Morning*
with equivalent charm, or accepting a leaflet

with anything other than a curt nod, or wandering
with any degree of interest to see the Becket Sword,
St George window, Sevastopol casualty lists.

If he raised his eyes at all to medieval glass
it would be to seek out old parishoners,
hill farmers at constant war with the bitter wind,

travelling, mystified, to Nativity or Crucifixion.
If he listened it would be to the conch shell
placed near an altar, recognising its translation

of an empty shore. If he prayed
it would be in those echoes of Amens
following a service. There he would

remember the untenanted chapels
he would visit returning from elsewheres
others overlooked. He never signed

visitors' books, finding the dried biro
too like a nail across damp paper, struggling
to make its mark. He never lit

candles for the dripped rack,
but marvelled rather that a draught
failed to extinguish lingering parables.

He was far more likely to stay outside,
intrigued by gulls, braving chilled April
sunlight that strangely followed Easter.

Gaze/Imagine

Another September; late afternoon, the medieval
sunlight sloping off from its side-altar duties;
an organ rehearsal of Handel repeats when a note trips,
resumes flourish, progresses. 'Gaze' a notice advises,

look on the High Altar, consider the significance
of Eucharist, as 'a way we somehow enter
the "being" of God' (that 'somehow' so Anglican),
and so read more deftly the East Window's stories –

crucifixion, resurrection, ascension. Who sketched
those faces the light drains drew memories from side-
    streets
where such soldiers loitered, and angels wondered,
as tomb sentries, how to explain things to fishermen.

Imagine it like the lit organ in an empty night-time,
island of sound; those shadows in Bach's Fugue.

Crow Music

We know they are not crows, yet
they exhibit crowness; the way they hang about,
painted, yet alert among medieval beams and lettering
in the old Prior's Tower. They roost
looking straight ahead. Yet we know
they are really peering over shoulders,
catching sight of confidential drafts
of the Chapter Minutes and listening in
to disclosures and confidences,

quotas, rotas, the music master's and architect's
reports being song-lines to them. Who knows,
after keys are turned, how they take flight,
sifting out between a crack in time
or transom, flapping black with their secrets,
dropping off hymn numbers like codes
for an advancing army?

Mass for Hands

The priest moves North, between the world and altar,
seeding each pair of hands with a circle of wafer,
a whole world, printed with a strung man dying for it.

She does not see their faces, just the ageing
of bowed heads brought to reverence near the candles;
the same fragility of light and shadow, the same

meekness for that moment, whoever they may be.
She knows their stories, reads them off their palms,
returns through remembered laughter, the embrace of
    weeping,

and further, into the stories she has told them
about the blind made clear, sowing and sheepfold,
this sharing through time, same lambing and reaping
    hands

now scrubbed for the service, still furrowed with trace of
    ground.
Stilled as the wafer is placed; patient for harvest.

Watching the Eucharist

We turned, as always at the end, from altar
towards the world, and found a line of people

had watched the Eucharist for Peace and Justice
while our backs were turned, setting the Military Chapel

in resurrection, restoring body and blood.
What had they seen? A man dressed in fine raiment

acting out text, lifting his hands, conducting
some sort of chamber music, without the music.

Sparse theatre; thinness among straight lines of chairs,
long reach among few people when they shook hands,

yet still that magnet to stay, still something ancient
becoming now; that drama where the audience

begins to act, where thought grows out of language,
and pausing is the energy from which we move.

Intentions

I walk this field for Jim. Our first encounter
came through an email from a mutual friend;
their years of walking tuned to Highland fitness,
the diagnosis told with his resilient smile.

As usual, from a writer, an old, old story
about Jim's typical march far side of a fell
while friends tagged after, gasping for a second wind.

I walk this winter field a thousandth time,
note pasture cropped tight, varnished with copper flakes
where beech leaves wedge in blades, the way the wall's

tumbled. I lift a few stones, click and lock
in gesture of rebuilding. Mist's cut off
firth's far-side, future country. Returning, pick

a birthday balloon, punctured of celebration,
a silver packet with its cancer warning,
a car park ticket with its time run out,

remember how each Mass has an intention,
also a medical term for healing wounds,
also a plan for marriage, or entering church.

No mid-day Mass today, instead four candles,
from different hours, form bar-code of petitions,
spread just a local light, flaring red sandstone.

Matches invite you, through parable and symbol,
to turn flame intercessory. Brisk, flagged footsteps
march to the stand; dropped clatter of an offering
leaves five flames spread, tallest of recent seeking,

catching the final words of Archibald Campbell
Tait's brass biography, Dean, Bishop, then Archbishop,
like titles I recall from internet chatting:
walker, grandfather, athlete; now a patient.

Something I'd never done before, the coin
clocked in the metal box; brief contacts –
the reach, the touch, the tilt, the spine of wax,
the catch of fire; the pause, before bowing out.

Postscript:
Wing

Somewhere, out among stars, a limping flight
takes her in circles, angel with a single wing,
always driven back by a siege engine of headwind,
stranger to the glory of host proclaiming Messiah.

Half-flight; lost wing restored in this half-timber
brought to light from a barn, given grace of vision
by this white geometry seasoned in unvarnished grain,
design as shoulder blade or scimitar at first glance.

Former life's still there like a beam in the eye,
square peg in a round hole, socket drilled open
for a bolt or dowel to pinion or ground fast;
a nail through the hand or foot to re-connect.

She might come looking, as we do, find the rest of her
as white design, goosedown, limestone or snow;
splintered current re-made as a rippling flight-beat,
slight wander of brushstroke made frayed leading edge.

She might drop a coin in the box, feel feathers stretch
with the glory of those balanced tiptoe in the altar window
when meeting the risen Christ. She'd duck through the
    door,
calculate angle of take-off to clear the fellside,
go, loosed again through the sheer air of completeness.

Notes and Acknowledgements

Most of these poems were written during a year as Poet in Residence at Carlisle Cathedral. Thanks are due to the Dean and Chapter for making possible this Residency, and to many people associated with the Cathedral who generously provided support, guidance and information.

Notes on individual poems

'Re-entering Afghanistan' is set in the Military Chapel, where the weekly Eucharist for Peace and Justice is celebrated.

'St Antony and the Projectionists' compares the faceless figures on the Cathedral panels about the saint's life with troops so badly disfigured in the First World War that they sought work alone, and in darkness, as cinema projectionists.

'Mirror' refers to the tilted mirror in the nave that reflects and magnifies the stars decorating the Cathedral roof.

'Estimating Zechariah' is based on the effigy of Bishop Samuel Waldegrave, and also refers to a sermon heard in the Outer Hebrides, on the prophecy of Zechariah, chapter one.

'Haiti' records the shelter built from egg boxes in Carlisle Cathedral to raise awareness of the victims of the devastating earthquake there.

'Olaf's Nativity' is imagined at the church dedicated to St Olaf, at Wasdale Head, Cumbria.

'Gaze/Imagine' draws on two of the pausing places on the Sensory Trail round the Cathedral.

'Wing' is based on a painting by Inigo Ford in St Michael and All Angels' Church, Nether Wasdale, Cumbria.

Thanks are due to the following publications, and media, where versions of, or extracts from, some of the poems first appeared: *ITV Border Television*, *BBC Radio Cumbria*, *Church Times*, *Cumberland News and Star*, *The Way*, *Carlisle Cathedral Bulletin*, *Manchester Cathedral Publications 2012*, and *Voicewalks*.

'Sanctuary' was nominated by *StepAway* magazine for the international Push Cart Prize (USA) in 2014.

Grateful thanks are due to Inigo Ford, for permission to reproduce as the cover illustration *Matthew Mark Luke and John No.1* (oil paint on wood: 52 cm x 80 cm x 8 cm), from a photograph by Jan Fialkowski (www.inigoford.co.uk).